THE MAGNETIC WOMAN'S GUIDE

Attract, Engage, and Keep the Man You Truly Desire

Randy B. Roark

Copyright © 2023 by Randy B. Roark

Other books by this Author

Table of content

Introduction

The Day Cupid Forgot My Address: Unveiling the Mysteries of Modern Love

My mascara stuck to my cheeks, echoing the shattered fragments of my heart. The rain outside wasn't only lamenting London's grey sky; it was echoing the tempest within me. Another failed blind date. Ten awful minutes, forced smiles like rusted hinges, and then the courteous retreat, leaving me drowning in the old anguish of loneliness.

Was this it? Was love merely a fairy tale told to naive girls in pink bedrooms? Was I condemned to forever negotiate the minefield of modern relationships, each false choice leading to another emotional crater?

That night, hidden in my attic flat, surrounded by books (my only genuine companions), I came across an old journal. It was leather-bound and worn, and it shouted promises of buried knowledge. It belonged to my Aunt Amelia, a lady who bucked tradition by choosing art above marriage, scandalizing the community with her fiery spirit and unrestrained heart.

A universe opened up as I gobbled her words. Tales of passionate loves and devastating goodbyes, of fiery independence and delicate sensitivity.

Amelia, it turned out, had written an epic love tale with her life, not on the blank pages of a diary, but on the canvas of time, with men as both the brushstrokes and the colours.

But it wasn't simply her narrative that drew me. It was the hidden map she'd weaved into her words, a guide to interpreting the male species (a secret society I badly desired to enter). She spoke of silent languages, emotional landscapes as intricate as the Colossus, and hidden wants and anxieties buried behind layers of societal expectations.

I set out on a quest, armed with Amelia's map and fuelled by my own broken heart. Not to find another date, but to comprehend the very essence of love, to navigate the often-turbulent seas of relationships with a compass of inquiry and a life raft of self-love.

This book is the conclusion of that trip, a fabric woven from Amelia's wisdom, my personal experiences, and the tales of numerous women I encountered along the road. It's a route plan for those of us who, like me, have stood at the crossroads of love, holding shattered dreams and questioning the very reality of happily ever afters.

We'll go on a journey to understand men, not as mythical beings or unachievable ideals, but as complex humans with their own set of aspirations, concerns, and emotional baggage. We'll decipher the cryptic language of communication, investigate the underlying motivations that drive their acts, and learn to communicate in a language they understand the language of respect, empathy, and vulnerability.

This novel does not guarantee a perfect prince or a storybook ending. It's a promise of self-discovery, of recognizing your power, and of navigating the world of relationships with grace, knowledge, and a good dose of levity.

So, ladies, take a deep breath, wipe away the mascara tears (we've all been there), and join me on this voyage. Let's dust off Aunt Amelia's map, reclaim our love tales, and rewrite the narratives of modern relationships one chapter, one understanding, one empowered step at a time.

Remember, the road to love may be paved with potholes and unexpected diversions, but with an open heart and a quest for knowledge, we can pave it with our resilience, laughter, and the wisdom imparted by generations of women who came before us.

Get ready, darlings, for it's time to turn the tables on love.

Who Should Read This?

This book bids a hearty welcome to:

- **The Inquiring Mind**: Are you sick of love's enigmas and eager to solve the puzzle? Do you want to comprehend men's emotional landscapes and navigate the often hazy seas of modern relationships? Then take your curiosity and dive in!

- **The Wanderer with a Broken Heart**: Have you tripped in the dating jungle, emerging with scratches and a shattered ego? This book is your salve, providing skills to help you heal, rebuild, and restore your faith in the game of love.

- **The Independent Spirit**: Do you want true connection without surrendering your individuality? This book celebrates your autonomy while also giving ideas for forming happy relationships that respect your beliefs and passions.

- **The Open-Minded Seeker**: Are you willing to let go of obsolete preconceptions and embrace a new viewpoint on men and relationships? This book embraces your willingness to learn, grow, and reinvent the story of love.

- **The Humor Enthusiast**: Life is too short for humourless travels! This book is sprinkled with fun and playful advice throughout, ensuring amusement while you negotiate the complexities of love.

This book may not be for you if:

- **You're Looking for Fairy Tales**: This book provides real-world observations rather than happily-ever-after fantasies. If you're looking for damsels in distress and Prince Charmings, you might find the realistic approach here a little too grounded.
- **You're a Closed Book**: This book thrives on openness and a willingness to learn. If you're entrenched in your ways and resistant to new ideas, you may miss out on crucial lessons.
- **You Want the Patriarchal Blueprint**: This book promotes equality and mutual respect. If you subscribe to traditional gender norms and expect males to fit a certain mould, you may find the content hard to your present belief system.
- **You are looking for quick fixes**: Building successful relationships requires time, effort, and self-reflection. This book is a road map, not a magic wand. If you're seeking quick fixes, you could find the path more complex than you expected.
- **You Take Offense Easily**: This book covers touchy themes with candour and wit. If you are easily offended by candid conversations about relationships and human nature, you should proceed with caution.

Chapter 1: Beyond Stereotypes: Demystifying the Male Mind and Emotional Landscape

Forget about stoic knights in dazzling armour and grunting cavemen. Men, in all their beautiful complexity, are not mythological beings hiding in a strange world. Understanding their particular wiring and emotional environment, on the other hand, might feel like reading *hieroglyphs* in the dark. But don't be alarmed, daring explorer! This chapter gives you the skills you need to break the code, destroy damaging preconceptions, and navigate the sometimes turbulent seas of male psychology.

Cracking the Code: How Men Think Differently

Let's get rid of the myth that men are soulless machines. Their brains, on the other hand, run somewhat different software. Men value rationality and problem-solving, and they frequently approach issues with a laser focus on finding an effective answer. This doesn't mean they don't have feelings; it just means their emotional processing may be more indirect. Remember that the lack of a weeping outburst does not imply disinterest. Pay attention to his behaviour, tone, and subtle adjustments in body language.

These are frequently the unnoticed entry points into their emotional universe.

Exploring Men's Emotional Depth

Think of an iceberg. The outward display of emotions is represented by the tip, which is visible above the water. But under the surface, there is a large, invisible universe of complicated emotions - fear, vulnerability, pride, and a need for connection that rivals your own. Don't confuse the austere exterior with a lack of depth. Their emotions, like the buried mass of an iceberg, are strong and influential. It is your responsibility to provide a secure environment in which they may feel at ease chipping away at that frigid veneer and unveiling the secret depths beneath.

Breaking Down the Barriers: Dispelling Common Men's Myths

Myths have an uncanny ability to distort our perspectives. So, let us shine some light on the most common:

1. **Myth No. 1 Men Do Not Require Intimacy**: False! Men, like women, need emotional connection. They may not always express it openly, but they need compassion, support, and a safe venue to express their weaknesses.

2. **Myth No. 2 Men Are Emotionally Immature**: Once again, false! They just express their feelings in

various ways. Recognize and appreciate their subtle clues and emotional language.

3. **Myth #3. Men Only Care About Sex**: Physical connection is important, but it is far from the only thing that men care about. Respect, true connection, and shared beliefs are all crucial components of a satisfying relationship for males.

Recognizing Triggers: Navigating Men's Emotional Landscape

Men, like everyone else, have emotional triggers. These triggers might range from criticism to feeling undervalued to working under stress. You may learn to approach circumstances with mindfulness and avoid unwittingly setting off alarms by learning what sets off your emotional barometer. Remember, honest communication is essential in this situation. Inquire gently about their triggers and collaborate to establish a safe environment where they may express themselves without fear of being judged.

Building Bridges: Communication Strategies for Deep Connections

A strong connection is built on effective communication. Drop the accusing tone, passive-aggressive suggestions, and cryptic statements to connect with a man. Speak, state your demands clearly, and most importantly, attentively listen.

Allow him to express himself freely and validate his feelings, even if you don't quite agree. Remember, comprehension does not imply agreement. You develop trust bridges and prepare the road for a deeper relationship by offering a secure place for open and honest discussion.

This is only the beginning of your adventure into the intriguing realm of the male psyche, my buddy. Men, like snowflakes, are individuals. Use these observations as a guide, not as a strict guideline. Celebrate their emotional complexity and, above all, approach them with inquiry, respect, and an open heart. You could just discover a treasure trove of love, understanding, and a partnership that transcends beyond the shallows of stereotypes and into the unfathomable depths of connection if you do so.

Chapter 2: What Men Want in Relationships: Beyond the Butterflies and Fireworks

The enticement of butterflies in your stomach and rockets exploding between you. But, let's be honest, the early spark of love, while exciting, seldom maintains a relationship through life's inevitable downpours. So, what keeps males in a relationship? What drives their devotion beyond the first spark of attraction? Dive deeper, my reader, as we peel back the layers to reveal the hidden gems lying within the masculine heart.

Beyond the Spark: Deeper Desires for Security and Companionship

Contrary to common assumption, males seek the same emotional anchors as women - a refuge of security and steadfast friendship. Consider it a robust oak providing shelter from life's storms. He craves a companion who feels like a haven, where weaknesses can be accepted, fears can be soothed, and laughter can be freely shared. This assurance comes from knowing you'll be at his side, a trusted confidante and steadfast support system, through thick and thin.

Shared Values, Shared Life: Aligning Your Future Visions

Imagine walking hand in hand down a twisting route, yet your destinations are miles away.

Misaligned values are like forks on the road, likely to lead to dissatisfaction and isolation. Men, like women, want a companion who shares their essential beliefs, the invisible threads that weave the fabrics of their lives. It is not about mirroring each other, but about appreciating and respecting one other's ambitions, objectives, and ethical compass. When your future aspirations collide, the route becomes one, paved with mutual understanding and steadfast support.

The Power of Respect: Fostering Trust and Mutual Understanding

Respect, the foundation of any lasting relationship, transcends words. It's woven into the fabric of your relationships, seen in your actions, decisions, and steadfast faith in each other. Men want partners who respect their individuality, accept their talents and flaws, and treat them with decency even when they disagree. Respect is not about mindless subservience; it is about developing trust via open conversation, active listening, and respecting each other's points of view. This rich basis of respect creates mutual understanding, which is the foundation for long-lasting love.

Speaking His Language: Identifying His Love Language and Effectively Expressing Affection

Words of affirmation, acts of service, receiving presents, quality time, and physical contact are the five love languages, each a distinct dialect in the emotional landscape. Recognize the language your boyfriend talks. Does he light up when you show your gratitude for his efforts? Does a shared journey speak volumes to his heart? Is a spontaneous cuddle more meaningful than a thousand elaborate gestures? Mastering his love language isn't about manipulating him; it's about expressing your devotion in a way that connects with him, fostering his emotional well-being, and demonstrating that he's genuinely understood.

Finding the Right Partner: Understanding His Relationship Goals

Not all men seek the same sanctuary amid the storm. Some people desire the security of a traditional relationship, while others thrive on the adventure of open partnerships. Some people want intellectual compatibility, while others seek a shared commitment to church or community. Understanding your man's relationship objectives - his dreams, anxieties, and expectations - is critical for ensuring you're both heading in the same direction. Open conversation, nonjudgmental investigation, and a willingness to comprehend his point of view are the instruments that illuminate the route to a happy partnership.

Remember, dear reader, that men are as different as snowflakes, each seeking a unique sanctuary in the tempest of the heart. By going beyond the brilliant pyrotechnics and understanding his underlying aspirations, you open the potential for a love that transcends brief pleasure and grows into a permanent, nurturing bond. Allow this chapter to serve as your compass, directing you toward a partnership in which both hearts discover their true north.

Chapter 3: The Art of Flirting and Attraction: Creating an Enduring Spark

Forget the damsels in distress and brave knights. Modern love relies on true connection, engaging exchanges, and the dance of mutual discovery. This chapter reveals the methods of sparking that early spark, growing it into a flame of shared desire, and constructing a bridge to lifelong closeness.

Embracing Your Authentic Self: Cultivating Confidence from Within

Forget the mask of perfection; it suffocates the compelling pull of authenticity. True confidence, the sort that attracts men like moths to a flame, isn't about concealing shortcomings, but about accepting your eccentricities, embracing your weaknesses, and exuding self-acceptance. It's not about bravado, but about understanding that you're enough exactly as you are. This inner confidence emits a bright radiance, a vulnerability that welcomes connection rather than judgment. Allow your laugh to ring genuine, your eyes to glitter with mischief, and your flaws to become your most alluring signature.

Mastering the Art of Flirting: Playful Communication and Lighthearted Connection

Flirting, the joyful dance of romance, isn't a formulaic checklist, but a spontaneous spark of wit, a teasing gaze across the room, a shared joke that leaves you both breathless with laughter. Get rid of the pick-up lines and planned routines. Instead, incorporate flirting into regular conversations. Allow your banter to flow naturally, grab his eye with a flirty wink, and sprinkle your chats with small hints of curiosity. Remember that humour is a powerful aphrodisiac; a well-timed remark may melt away shyness and kindle the simmering fires of passion.

Recognizing Your Vulnerability: Building Trust and Intimacy

Love needs vulnerability, not an unyielding fortress. Sharing your concerns, dreams, and insecurities is not a sign of weakness, but rather a gateway to a deeper relationship. Trust is created brick by brick by creating a secure area for him to open his own heart. It's in the quiet times of exchanging secrets whispered at twilight that you genuinely touch his spirit and kindle a link that goes beyond the surface. Don't be afraid of vulnerability; embrace it as the entrance to genuine closeness, the fertile ground where love may thrive.

Finding Common Ground: Exploring Shared Interests and Passion

Common passions produce common sparks. Dive into researching mutual interests, the playgrounds where you may learn and grow together. When you bring up art, does his face light up? Plan a museum tour beneath the stars. Does talking about music make his pulse race? Play your favourite music and dance like no one is looking. Remember that shared experiences weave threads of connection, establishing a sense of belonging and expanding the fabric of your tie.

Keeping the Spark Alive: Creative Ways to Stay Playful and Connected

Love isn't a stagnant pool; it's a raging river that's continuously looking for fresh tributaries. Keep the lively spirit alive with unexpected excursions, such as an impromptu picnic in the park, a late-night stargazing session, or a cooking lesson where you giggle over burned offerings and flour-dusted cheeks. Make dates a priority, but avoid the tired dinner-and-a-movie routine. Embrace spontaneity, arrange surprises, and inject adventure into your lives together. Remember that even the tiniest flame needs oxygen to survive. With inventiveness, fun curiosity, and a mutual desire for new experiences, you may fan the flames of passion.

This chapter, my reader, is your instruction manual for lighting the initial spark and fanning it into a raging fire. Remember that attraction thrives on sincerity, vulnerability, and playful connection. Embrace your genuine self, appreciate mutual interests, and keep the spirit of adventure alive. You will not only kindle the first flame, but also foster a friendship that will last, fuelled by laughter, mutual understanding, and an ever-evolving adventure of discovery.

Chapter 4: Communication Secrets: Unlocking Commitment and Nurturing Love

Words, my reader, are not merely stones scattered in the wind. They are the bridge builders, the trust weavers, and the navigators of love's undiscovered waters. This chapter reveals the keys to good communication, the very lifeblood of a flourishing relationship, bringing you toward commitment, understanding, and enduring love.

The Power of Listening: Actively Understanding His Point of View

Consider holding a valuable diamond, but instead of enjoying its facets, you just concentrate on refining your reflection. Listening, actually listening, is focusing on him. Active listening is delving into his words, absorbing his feelings, and attempting to grasp the world through his eyes. Nod, paraphrase, and ask clarifying questions. Silence your mental chatter and be present in the echo of his thoughts. In that moment of careful listening, you develop trust bridges, generating a sense of comfort and connection that whispers a silent *"I am here for you."*

Expressing Your Needs: Effective Communication for Mutual Fulfillment

Clarity, not cryptic declarations, is the key to conveying your desires. Stop using passive-aggressive hints and accusing tones. Speak your truth directly, yet with respect. Tell him what you require, what makes you feel loved and respected. This is not about making demands, but about cultivating mutual understanding. Remember, guys cannot read thoughts (as much as we wish they could!). Be your advocate, explain your desires clearly and honestly, and watch as those open doors lead to meaningful partnerships where both needs are addressed, creating an orchestra of shared delight.

Setting Healthy Boundaries: Maintaining Respect and Individuality

Love grows on mutual respect, and respect blooms in the fertile soil of healthy limits. These are not walls of isolation, but fences that defend your originality and sense of self. Communicate your dealbreakers or the non-negotiables that characterize your basic convictions. Learn to say "*no*" politely, prioritize your well-being, and refuse to accept disrespect. Healthy limits aren't selfish; they're the foundation of a relationship founded on mutual trust and understanding when two lively individuals choose to come together rather than lose themselves in the process.

Maintaining Openness and Honesty: Building Trust Through Transparent Communication

Honesty is not a one-time gift; it is a continuous offering on the altar of trust. Be open and honest about your insecurities, concerns, and even foolish blunders. Remember that keeping secrets is like hanging on to a flaming ember; it will only harm you in the long run. Accept genuineness, express your truth even if it's painful, and trust him to carry your vulnerability with care. Trust flourishes in the bright space of honesty, providing a refuge where hearts can securely beat as one, unburdened by the shadows of lying.

Navigating Disagreements: Healthy Conflict Resolution Strategies

Disagreements aren't disasters to be avoided; they're chances for progress. Approach them in a collaborative, rather than combative, manner. Get rid of the blame game, the nasty jabs, and the emotional landmines. Instead, listen politely, accept his point of view, and attempt to discover solutions that meet both of your requirements. Focus on *"we" rather than "me,"* seek common ground, and compromise without abandoning your essential convictions. Remember that effective conflict resolution isn't about winning or losing; it's about developing a stronger, more resilient connection, brick by brick, via honest talk and mutual understanding.

This chapter, my reader, is your instruction manual for weaving the silky threads of communication into the fabrics of your love. Remember that good communication is a tango, not a solitary effort. Listen actively, communicate your needs, cultivate respect via healthy limits, and walk the bright road of honesty. As you manage conflicts with compassion and understanding, you will not only unleash commitment but also nurture a love that can withstand any storm, fed by the rich nectar of clear and open communication.

Chapter 5: Recognizing What Men Require: Fueling His Fire and Celebrating His Journey

Men, like great oak trees, need more than simply sunlight and moisture to grow. Their hearts are filled with longing, not for damsels in distress, but for companions who light their pathways, feed their dreams, and celebrate their journeys. This chapter looks into men's underlying desires, leading you to become more than simply a lover, but a growth partner, a champion of his aspirations, and a co-architect of a shared future.

Recognizing and Supporting His Unspoken Needs

Contrary to common assumption, men are not stoic success machines. They have hopes, anxieties, and vulnerabilities hidden under a tough exterior. Become a sharp observer of his emotions and concerns and a detective of his unsaid wants. What makes his eyes sparkle when he speaks? What difficulties motivate him? Listen carefully, provide constant support, and act as his confidante in the pursuit of his goals. Instead of trying to shape him into your ideal, celebrate his uniqueness, support his unique path, and be the wind under his wings as he flies towards his own Everest.

Celebrating Successes: Promoting His Development and Offering Praise

A pat on the back and a hearty "good job" aren't just meaningless gestures; they're rain showers that fertilize his parched confidence seed. Every time he summits a peak, let your love be a symphony of encouragement, a chorus of applause. Recognize his efforts, celebrate his tiny and large achievements, and provide genuine praise that warms his spirit like the midday sun. Remember that men need affirmation for their everyday conflicts and lessons learnt, not simply their spectacular triumphs. Be his steadfast cheerleader, his voice of belief, and watch as your encouragement ignites his quest to become the finest version of himself.

The Appreciation Effect: Expressing Gratitude and Creating Value

Appreciation isn't just a passing praise; it's a powerful fertilizer that grows a man's feeling of worth. Take his love, support, and efforts for granted. Express your thanks in regular quiet moments, not just huge gestures. A genuine *"thank you" for making you laugh, fixing that leaking faucet, or simply being there has an enormous impact.* Remember that for males, feeling appreciated serves as an emotional oxygen mask. Recognize his efforts, emphasize his talents, and allow your gratitude to build a vivid image of how much he means to you.

Embracing Individuality: Maintaining Personal Passions and Growth

Love does not need assimilation; it lives on the symphony of uniqueness. Encourage him to pursue his interests and activities that make his soul sing. Celebrate his solitary trips, time with friends, and interests that bring him delight outside of the common area rather than clipping his wings in the cause of unity. Remember that a fulfilled person makes a gratifying spouse. Be his haven for exploration, his cheerleader for personal development, and watch as your appreciation for his uniqueness creates a sense of trust and mutual admiration.

Setting Shared Goals: Creating a Vision for Your Future Together

Love is a ship moving towards a common horizon, not merely a warm sanctuary. Set long-term and short-term goals that fuel your joint ambitions as you chart your future together. Let your dreams connect, weaving a connection of shared purpose, whether you're building a dream house, exploring the globe, or starting a family. Remember that working for a common objective generates a sense of cooperation, of being in this together rather than merely side by side. Dream big, plan together, and celebrate your accomplishments along the way, and you'll be on your way to a future as bright and rewarding as the love that connects you.

This section is your guide to uncovering the secret terrain of his aspirations, dear reader. Remember, men need support, not suffocation; encouragement, not criticism; and recognition, not apathy. Be his storm anchor, his wind in his sails, and his beacon of hope. Celebrate his achievements, cultivate his uniqueness, and create a future filled with the brilliant colours of shared ambitions and unflinching support. You will not only discover the keys to knowing what men require, but you will also create a relationship that lives on mutual respect, growth, and the intoxicating delight of navigating life's journeys as one.

Chapter 6: Weathering the Storm: Tools for Effective Communication and Conflict Resolution

Love's journey isn't a calm lake; it's a raging river, sometimes meandering serenely, boiling with rapids. Conflict, like those rapids, is unavoidable; it is not a sign of failure. This aspect provides you with the oars and life vests you need to cross these treacherous waters, emerging not only uninjured, but closer, stronger, and ready to weather any storm together.

Communication Strategies for Healthy Disagreements: Emotional Expression in a Positive Way

Consider attempting to extinguish a fire using gasoline. Yelling, blaming, and emotional grenades only serve to fuel the fires of confrontation. Use communication techniques to put out the fire. *Speak in "I" statements, expressing yourself without reproach.* Listen actively, rather than defending your own. Recognize his feelings, accept his right to feel differently, and resist the desire to dismiss his experiences. Remember, constructive disputes aren't about winning or losing; they're about navigating towards a greater knowledge of each other and the process of conflict resolution.

Finding Win-Win Solutions: Collaborating on Compromise and Growth

Compromise isn't a half-eaten pizza where one individual selects their preferred toppings while leaving the dough for the other. Compromise is a shared feast in successful partnerships, with each person contributing ingredients and savouring the resulting flavours. Approach disputes as a group, not as opponents. Rather than digging trenches, brainstorm solutions together. Be willing to bend, to adapt, to find that happy medium where all of your wants are addressed, resulting in a sweeter, more nutritious ending for both of you. Remember that real compromise honours development rather than sacrifice.

Rebuilding After Conflict: Repairing Damage and Strengthening Trust

Every storm leaves debris in its wake. Clear the debris of angry words and lose trust once the battle has died down. Accept responsibility for your actions, make genuine apologies for any sins, and actively seek forgiveness. Don't linger on previous mistakes; instead, concentrate on improving the present. Initiate reconciliation, participate in open conversation, and restore trust one empathic brick at a time. Remember that forgiving is not forgetting; it is choosing to move forward together, bearing the lessons learned but not the wounds of struggle.

Maintaining Respect and Understanding: Embracing Diversity and Open Communication

Love does not require clones; rather, it thrives on the mosaic of individuality. You'll have various points of view, different priorities, and different ways of looking at the world. Respect his point of view, even if it differs from yours. Encourage open communication and a secure atmosphere where vulnerabilities may be discussed and worries can be expressed without judgement. Remember that genuine understanding does not eliminate differences; it bridges them, erecting a bridge of empathy and acceptance that allows you to connect on a deeper level, despite the unique shapes of your landscapes.

Evolving Communication Styles: Adapting to Change and Growth

Communication methods, like rivers, change throughout time. What works originally may need to be tweaked as you progress through the phases of your relationship, personal growth, and external problems. Be open to changing your communication ways, learning his new love languages, and getting outside help if necessary. Remember that communication is a dynamic dance, not a rigid posture. Embrace the ebb and flow, the need for learning and adaptation, and watch as your capacity to connect deepens and blooms, keeping your love story both alive and resilient.

This chapter, dear reader, isn't only a how-to guide for surviving storms; it's also a compass for sailing towards calmer seas. Remember, disagreement is an opportunity, not a danger. Equip yourself with effective communication tools, cooperate on ideas, repair trust after conflicts, and enjoy the never-ending dance of adaptability. You'll not only weather any storm that life throws your way, but you'll deepen your relationship, create a haven of understanding, and emerge from each hardship closer, stronger, and more in love than ever before.

Bonus Section: 30 Things Guys Wish Girls Knew (Beyond "Men Need Love and Acknowledgment")

1. **Vulnerability is Strength**: We are not stoic machines. We all have fears, doubts, and dreams that we want to convey. Sometimes simply knowing you're there to listen without judgment is enough.
2. **Respect Our Silence:** Sometimes we just need to digest things inwardly. Allow us to unwind without requiring explanations. In those moments, a subtle presence may say a lot.
3. **Communication is a Two-Way Street**: Actively listen, ask follow-up questions, and seek to comprehend our point of view. We attempted to understand you, so please return the favour.
4. **Recognize Our Efforts**: A simple "thank you" for repairing that leaking faucet or bringing out the garbage goes a long way. Recognizing our modest acts of kindness drives our desire to keep doing them.
5. **We Pay Attention to Details**: A fresh haircut, an item of favourite clothing, a genuine smile - we pay attention to details, and your gratitude is appreciated.
6. **We Want Adventure**: Don't simply arrange dinner dates. Surprising us with spontaneous trips,

weekend vacations, or exploring new things together. Keep life exciting, and we'll be eager to be with you.

7. **Encourage Our Activities**: Whether it's gaming, music, or tinkering with vehicles, show real interest in our activities. Encourage us even if you don't entirely comprehend what we're saying.

8. **Affirmation is Powerful**: Tell us you're proud of us, that you find us beautiful, and that you enjoy our sense of humour. Your words of encouragement have had a significant influence on our confidence and self-esteem.

9. **Physical Touch Is Important**: A hug, a handshake, a playful nudge - physical closeness expresses affection and enhances our friendship. Don't underestimate the power of a mere touch.

10. **Be Our Partners, Not Competitors**: We thrive on cooperation and collaboration. Support our aims, celebrate our victories, and be our cheerleaders, not our competitors.

11. **We Can Be Messy Too**: Don't expect us to be flawlessly groomed domestic goddesses. Let us have our eccentricities and sloppy moments. Life is messy, and we are, too, in a lovely way.

12. **Respect Our Independence**: We enjoy our alone time and require room to explore our particular interests.

Trust that we can be joyful and whole even when we aren't tied to your hip.

13. **Don't Play Mind Games**: We're not detectives attempting to understand cryptic clues. Be forthright, talk honestly, and state your wants plainly. Mixed messages and passive-aggressive methods only lead to frustration.

14. **Communication Styles Differ**: We may not always communicate ourselves in the same way that you do. Recognize our distinct communication styles and be patient if it takes us a bit longer to express our feelings.

15. **We Value Honesty**: Even if it's uncomfortable, give us the truth, even if it's not what you think we want to hear. Honesty, especially when it is difficult, is the foundation of respect and trust.

16. **We Can Be Sensitive, too**: Yes, we have feelings! Don't underestimate our emotional strength. Words may be hurtful, so treat our vulnerabilities with care and respect.

17. **Respect Our Uniqueness**: Don't try to change us into your ideal guy. Appreciate our eccentricities, sense of humour, and the distinctive characteristics that make us who we are.

18. **Laughter is the Best Medicine**: Tell jokes, make funny expressions, and don't take yourself too

seriously. A good dosage of humour may lift our spirits and improve our relationship.

19. **We Have Feelings About Our Bodies**: We, too, are self-conscious about our physical appearance. Compliments are always appreciated, and mild encouragement goes a long way.

20. **We Can Feel Intimidated, Too:** Don't always portray an image of unwavering confidence. It's normal to be vulnerable, to seek support, and to share your fears. We can connect to that more than you would imagine.

21. **We Dream of the Future, Too**: Share your dreams, objectives, and long-term plans. We want to know where you want to go and be a part of the trip.

22. **Show Us You Trust Us**: Allow us to make errors, learn from them, and develop. Don't micromanage or continually second-guess our judgments. A solid connection is built on trust.

23. **We Need to Forgive Each Other**: Holding grudges and previous hurts only builds distance. Be willing to forgive, move on, and focus on creating a better future.

24. **Recognize the Power of Silence**: Sometimes the most expressive words are left unsaid. Learn to embrace comfortable silences, when unspoken understanding and a shared presence fill the gap between words.

25. **We Can Be Creatively Expressive, Too**: Don't assume we're all stern and emotionless. We can express ourselves via music, painting, literature, or even acts of service. Pay attention to these subtle manifestations of our inner world.

26. **Celebrate Our Inner Child**: Have fun and accept stupid times. Don't be afraid to be lively, spontaneous, and a little silly. We value couples who can laugh at themselves and enjoy life's basic joys.

27. **Be Our Safe Haven**: A partnership should be a haven from the storms of life. Show us you're a safe place where we can be vulnerable, communicate our fears, and know we'll be welcomed with compassion and understanding.

28. **Communication Isn't Just Words**: Actions speak louder than words. Show us how much you care by your deeds, both big and small. A thoughtful gesture, a helpful hand, or simply being present may tell volumes about your love and dedication.

29. **We Want to Learn and Grow, Too**: Share your information, experiences, and viewpoints with us. Challenge us intellectually, introduce us to new ideas, and assist us in becoming better versions of ourselves. We develop best when we learn and explore together.

30. **Love Comes in Many Forms**: Don't attempt to shoehorn our love story into a preset mould. Allow it

to evolve naturally, expressing itself in unique ways that resonate with both of us. Remember that love is a journey, not a destination, and that enjoying its various manifestations is essential for a happy relationship.

Remember, they are only glances into the complicated inner world of man. Understanding your relationship will involve attentive listening, careful observation, and open and honest communication. However, by identifying these common goals and accepting individual differences, you may create a partnership that is not only filled with love and acknowledgement, but also with mutual respect, understanding, and a joyous path of growth together.

Chapter 7: Building a Lasting Connection: The Everlasting Bridge of Love

Love, like a wonderful suspension bridge, thrives on firm foundations. This chapter digs into the vital pillars that keep that bridge afloat, guiding you towards a love that is more than a transient flame, but a beacon of shared ideals, steadfast trust, and continual progress, illuminating your path together even as life's winds and seas dance around you.

Aligning Your Compass: Identifying Shared Values and Creating a Foundation for the Future

Consider two ships starting sail, each with a distinct destination. Shared values are the guiding lights that keep your ships on course. Examine the basic ideas that serve as the foundation of your individual lives: respect, honesty, loyalty, kindness, family values, financial perspectives, spirituality - are these threads woven into the fabric of your common vision? Discuss openly, seek common ground, and enjoy your tapestries, enabling them to interweave into a colourful vision for the future you'll create together. Remember that shared values aren't about carbon-copy conformity; they're about finding the harmonic junction where your separate paths connect, creating a solid foundation for your love story to unfold.

Building Trust Through Transparency: Vulnerability, Honesty, and Emotional Openness

Trust, the unseen bridge truss, bears the weight of love's deepest feelings. Maintain it by being completely transparent. Vulnerability is not a weakness; it is the raw bravery to reveal your concerns, anxieties, and ambitions. Share your feelings openly, convey your needs honestly, and offer a safe environment for him to do the same. Remember that secrets are chains that weigh down trust. Be each other's confidantes, embrace open communication, and watch as trust, brick by vulnerable brick, forms an impenetrable fortress for your love to bloom inside.

Embracing Change and Growth: Adapting to Life's Challenges Together

Life's tides put even the strongest bridges to the test. Challenges, like unforeseen storms, will unavoidably upset your ship. However, keep in mind that adaptation is the lifeblood of resilience. Support each other through choppy waters, tackle hurdles together, and manage uncertainty with open communication and steadfast trust in your connection. Celebrate individual development, inspire new goals, and serve as one other's anchors amid stormy seas. Remember that a partnership that weathers storms together emerges stronger, its foundation strengthened by shared resilience and the reassuring awareness that you confront the world as a unified front.

Continual Learning and Development: Keeping the Relationship Dynamic and Fresh

Stagnation is the enemy of passion. Continued study and personal growth will keep the flames of curiosity burning strong. Accept new experiences together, venture into unexplored territory, and be each other's cheerleaders while you follow your distinct hobbies. Attend workshops, travel to new places, engage in fascinating conversations, and intellectually push yourself. Remember that a dynamic relationship is a playground of discovery, where you not only learn and grow as people but also rediscover each other, keeping the spark of excitement alive in your shared world.

Nurturing Love and Intimacy: Maintaining Passion and Connection as a Team

Love, like a fragile flower, requires regular attention. Don't let familiarity overpower intimacy. Plan romantic trips, rediscover the delight of physical contact, and whisper sweet nothings beneath a starlit sky. Celebrate large and little events, and communicate your love in a variety of ways - spectacular gestures, thoughtful acts of service, whispered praises, and lighthearted banter.

Remember that intimacy whispers in the quiet moments, grows in shared laughter, and burns in the fires of shared desire. Keep the fire burning and watch as your love story evolves, a brilliant bond woven with strands of romance, shared adventures, and the soothing warmth of unbroken closeness.

This chapter, dear reader, is more than a blueprint; it's a compass for navigating the ever-changing terrain of love. Remember that shared values are the guiding stars, trust is the bridge's solid truss, and adaptation is its resilient mast. Accept ongoing growth, reignite the embers of closeness, and tackle life's obstacles together. As you cultivate these foundations, your love will not only endure but will change into a stunning tribute to the enduring strength and beauty of a connection founded on shared aspirations, unflinching support, and the intoxicating thrill of navigating life's path as one.

Conclusion: The End of a Love Story

The final page flutters close, leaving echoes of shared laughter, hushed vulnerabilities whispered beneath the starlight and the exciting dance of navigating life's journeys together. This book, dear reader, was more than simply a collection of words; it was a love tale, a tapestry woven with strands of understanding, support, and the seductive optimism that bonds two souls in an endless desire for connection.

Throughout these chapters, we walked through the maze alleyways of attraction, constructed communication bridges across stormy streams of conflict, and nursed the delicate orchid of intimacy in the lush soil of shared ideals and unflinching trust. We investigated men's underlying desires, welcomed the power of vulnerability, and accepted the continual transformation of growth, both individually and as a group.

Remember, this was a blueprint, a whisper in the wind pointing you to a love tale richer and more colourful than any chronicled on these pages. The ink may dry, and the cover may close, yet the adventure continues. Carry the lessons learnt into the fabric of your relationship, adapt them to the specific rhythm of your love song, and let them be the compass that directs you through sunlight and storm.

If these words struck a chord with you, if they triggered a flash of recognition in the mirror of your own experiences, consider this a tiny request. Leave a review, a ripple in the virtual world's pond, a murmured testament that this story made its way into your heart. Your voice, when shared with others, might be the compass that guides another wandering soul to the bright refuge of a love story waiting to be written.

So, my reader, go forth and compose your own. Allow vulnerability to be your ink, shared aspirations to be your canvas, and steadfast support to be the brushstrokes that create a masterpiece of connection that transcends the conclusion of this book and resonates in the symphony of your love's never-ending journey.